OUR • WORLD • MY • ROOTS

KENYA

WRITTEN BY ANNA MAKANDA & SHARMANE BARRETT

ILLUSTRATED BY NATÀLIA JUAN ABELLÓ

OUR DEDICATIONS

In Anna's words:

To my parents, for always believing in me and encouraging me to shoot for the moon. To my mum, for teaching me that in order to know who you are, you must know where you come from. To my husband, for being my absolute rock through thick and thin. To my two beautiful children, who inspire me every day.

In Sharmane's words:

To my parents and my sisters for being my biggest challengers, as well as supporters, in life. To my ten amazing nieces and nephews, for being my constant reminder that I need to be a better me for all of the little eyes that are watching.

To all the little explorers,
may you always remember to:

BE CURIOUS

BE CONFIDENT

BE KIND

BE YOU

CONTENTS

NORTH AMERICA

EUROPE

AFRICA

SOUTH AMERICA

KENYA

ANTARCTICA

LOCATION

Kenya is a country in East Africa. It is bordered by five countries. South Sudan and Ethiopia are to the north, Somalia and the Indian Ocean are to the east, and Tanzania is to the south. Uganda and Lake Victoria are to the west.

Size: 224,081 mi²
Capital: Nairobi 🔍
Currency: Kenyan shilling (KES)
Population: 52.4 million (2024)
Major Cities: Mombasa, Kisumu, Nakuru and Eldoret 🔍
Highest Point: Batian Peak, Mount Kenya at 5,199 m 🔍

WEATHER

Kenya has three types of climate: hot and humid along the coast, temperate in the west and south-west (where there are mountains and plateaus), and hot and dry in the north and east. Temperatures range from 50 to 104 degrees Fahrenheit.

LANGUAGES

Swahili and English are the official languages of Kenya, but there are 68 languages spoken. The main language groups are Bantu, Nilotic and Cushitic. Swahili is a Bantu language, and there are many dialects of the Swahili language.

RELIGION

85% of the Kenyan population are Christian, and 11% are Muslim. The remaining 4% practice other faiths including Baha'i, Buddhism, Hinduism and traditional religions.

ASIA

OCEANIA

KEEP AN EYE OUT FOR

🔍 Capital: Nairobi
🔍 Major Cities: Mombasa, Kisumu, Nakuru and Eldoret
🔍 Mountains: Mount Kenya, Mount Elgon and Mount Satima
🔍 Rivers: Tana River, Ewaso Ng'iro River
🔍 Lake Victoria
🔍 Nyahururu Waterfall
🔍 Lamu Old Town
🔍 Gedi Ruins
🔍 Nairobi National Park

LAKE VICTORIA

LAKE TURKANA

CHALBI DESERT

GREAT RIFT VALLEY

KAISUT DESERT

MOUNT ELGON

EWASO NG'IRO

ELDORET

NAKURU

MOUNT KENYA

KISUMU

TANA

MOUNT SATIMA

LAMU OLD TOWN

MAASAI MARA

NAIROBI

LAKE MAGADI

GEDI RUINS

MOMBASA

INDIAN OCEAN

ARE YOU EXCITED ABOUT GOING ON AN ADVENTURE?

Join us on a journey across land and sea, taking you to Kenya: the land of unparalleled raw beauty, often referred to as the "Jewel of East Africa." It is a country that holds a multitude of thrilling treasures; Mother Nature's magnificence never fails to capture hearts and minds. This book will guide you through the country's geography, people, culture, and beyond.

But there's more there than meets the eye: Kenya has an array of languages, communities, beliefs and traditions. The people of Kenya are known for being very kind. Hakuna matata means "no worries" - a philosophy held dearly by most Kenyans. They do not stress too much about things they cannot change, and they are spirited yet humble people. You may be surprised to find that even though Kenya has lots of things that are different to where you live, there are many similarities too.

Kenya is approximately 17 times smaller than the USA and home to over 51 million people who speak many languages.

Perhaps you have Kenyan heritage and you want to learn more about your roots, or simply want to learn more about this amazing country. You will find some of the many special things about Kenya in this book, but there is so much more to discover. We hope that someday you will be able to travel all the way to Kenya and beyond.

THE OFFICIAL LANGUAGES OF KENYA ARE SWAHILI AND ENGLISH. THIS IS HOW TO SAY "HELLO" IN THREE OF THE OTHER WIDELY SPOKEN LANGUAGES.

HELLO

HABARI
(SWAHILI)

Some of the other languages are:
Luhya, Bukusu, Kalenjin and Somali.

DHOLUO
(MISAWA)

KAMBA
(ÛVOOWAKU)

KIKUYU
(WI MWEGA)

Throughout the pages of this book you will
find many words and phrases translated in:
Swahili (blue)

HI, WELCOME TO KENYA.

MY NAME IS KAMAU
AND I AM 9 YEARS OLD.

THIS IS MY YOUNGER SISTER,
AMANI. SHE IS 6 YEARS OLD.

AND THESE ARE MY BEST FRIENDS:
MWANGI WHO IS 8, AND ZURI,
WHO IS THE SAME AGE AS ME.

WE ARE REALLY EXCITED
TO SHOW YOU AROUND...

LET'S BEGIN OUR ADVENTURE!

MEET MY FAMILY

I live with my parents and my two sisters: Amani and Naiya. We live in Narok.
We speak Swahili and English. I have many aunts, uncles and cousins too,
who live in different areas in Kenya. Let me introduce you to my...

Family
Familia

Mom
Mama

Dad
Baba

Brother
Kaka

Sister
Dada

Grandad
Babu

Grandma
Bibi

Cousin
Binamu

Uncle
Mjomba

Auntie
Shangazi

Friend
Rafiki

MWANGI AND ZURI'S FAMILY ALSO LIVE IN NAROK, THEY ALSO SPEAK SWAHILI AND ENGLISH.

My parents and Mwangi's parents are good friends as our dads do business together. We call Mwangi's mom "Mama" and his dad "Mzee." In general, we call adults "Shangazi" (Auntie) or "Mjomba" (Uncle). Mama says this is the way we show our respect to those who are older than us.

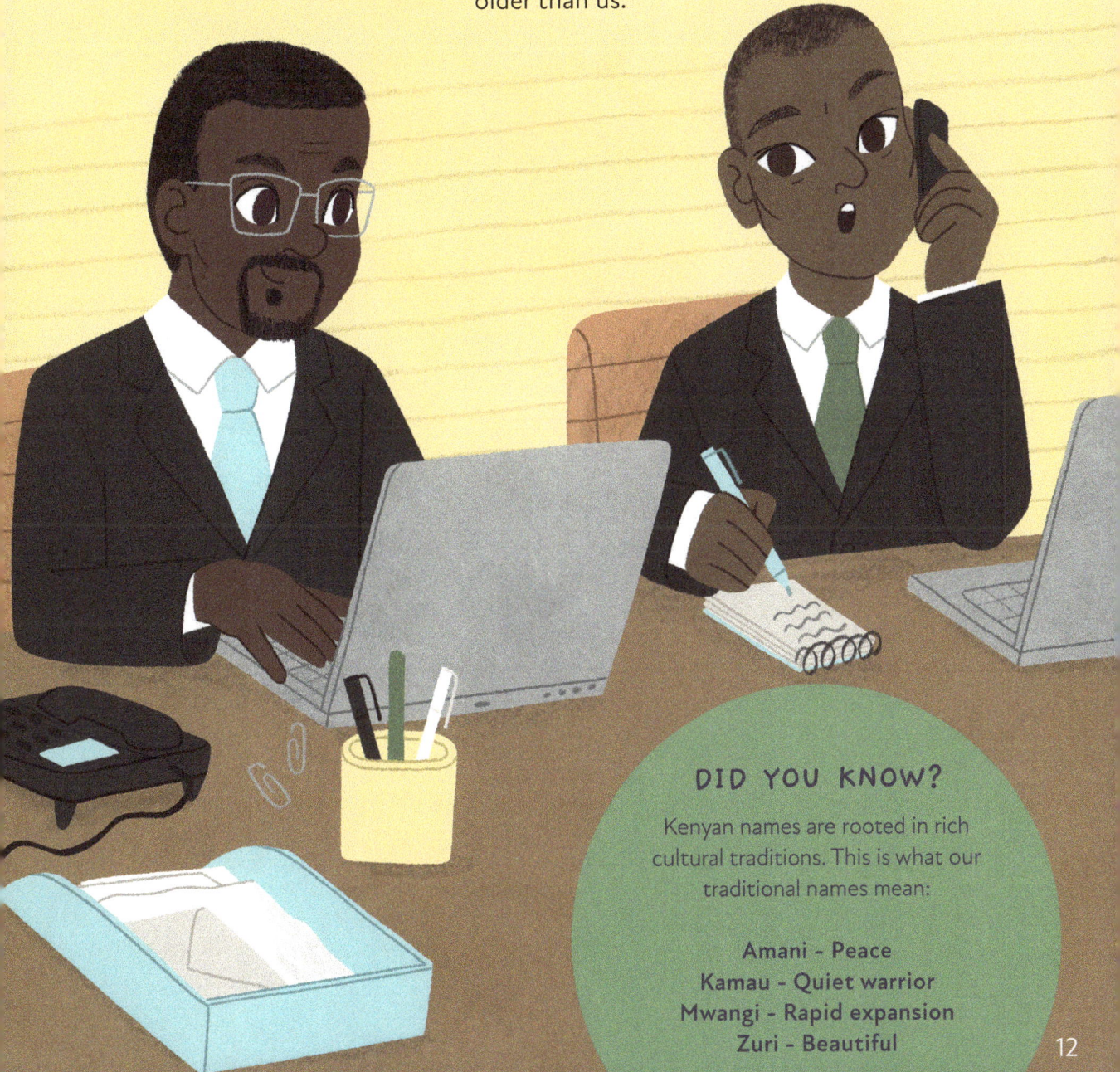

DID YOU KNOW?

Kenyan names are rooted in rich cultural traditions. This is what our traditional names mean:

Amani - Peace
Kamau - Quiet warrior
Mwangi - Rapid expansion
Zuri - Beautiful

WHERE WE LIVE

Traditionally, Bantu speakers mainly lived in the south. The Kikuyu, Kamba, Meru and Nyika people occupied the Central Rift highlands, and the Luhya and Gusii inhabit the Lake Victoria basin. Today, there is a lot more mixing between cultural groups across Kenya.

Amani and I live in an apartment in Narok. Mwangi and Zuri live in the same apartment block as us. Our apartment is small, but it has running water and electricity.

Home
Nyumbani

My cousins, Baraka, Omari and Akinyi live in a large settlement in Mukuru, which is in Nairobi. The settlement has 21 neighborhoods. Their home is just one room. It's made of corrugated iron and so is the roof.

Our cousins Kiptoo and Nduta live in a big town house in Karen, which is in Nairobi.

DID YOU KNOW?

There is a village known as Umoja Uaso, founded in the 1990s, where only women and children are allowed to live.

LET'S EXPLORE

LANDSCAPES

Amani and I love visiting different parts of Kenya to see family.
Sometimes Mama and Baba take us all on a long bus ride, or on
the train so we can visit somewhere new. It is such an adventure.
Here are some of the things we see when we explore...

Explore
Chunguza

MOUNTAINS Q

Kenya is renowned for its impressive
mountain ranges. The three largest are:

Mount Kenya

(the second largest in Africa)

Mount Elgon

Mount Satima

RIVERS Q

Kenya is home to a multitude of rivers coursing
through its landscapes. The two main ones are:

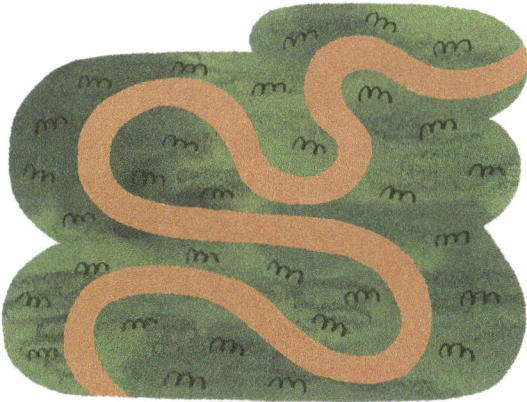

The Tana River, Kenya's 'beating heart', is the
deepest and longest river in Kenya. It starts in
the highlands of central Kenya and flows north
eastward into the Indian Ocean.

**Q: How many leopards would fit along
the length of the Tana River?
A: 633,750 leopards – it's 630 m long**

The Ewaso Ng'iro River also begins in
the highlands of central Kenya and flows
northward through forests, grasslands and
wetlands, emptying into the Lorian Swamp.

**Q: How many elephants would fit
along the length of the Ewaso Ng'iro?
A: 116,667 elephants – it's 435 m long**

GREAT RIFT VALLEY

The great rift valley is located along the East African rift, where two tectonic plates are moving apart (essentially breaking the continent in two). It cuts through the continent from Ethiopia to Mozambique, right through the middle of Kenya. There is extensive volcanic activity here, and huge lakes form in the area.

LAKES Q

There are more than 64 lakes in Kenya, eight of which are found within Kenya's Great Rift Valley. Most of them are natural lakes, but a few are man-made reservoirs. Some are big and deep, some are small and shallow. Lake Turkana is the world's largest desert lake, and Lake Victoria is Africa's largest lake. It is shared by three countries: Kenya, Uganda and Tanzania. Kenya's lakes are a great spot for viewing wildlife. You can expect to see many animals hanging out at their favorite watering hole.

DID YOU KNOW?

Kenya is home to one of the world's most mesmerizing natural wonders: a pink lake! Lake Magadi is known for its beautiful pink color, which is caused by high levels of salt and minerals in the water that flows from hot springs.

WATERFALLS 🔍

There are more than 20 stunning waterfalls in Kenya,
including the famous Nyahururu (Thomson) Falls,
referred to as nature's masterpiece, the scenic Karuru Falls,
the mesmerizing Fourteen Falls and the hidden treasures
of Chania Falls.

Karuru Falls

Fourteen Falls

Chania Falls

PLATEAUS

A plateau is an area of flat land with a steep slope on at least one side. Kenya has six plateaus: Laikipia, Nyika, Kinangop, Yatta, East African and Central plateau.

DID YOU KNOW?

Laikipia has a high concentration of endangered species; it is home to the two last remaining northern white rhinos, Fatu and Najin.

SAVANNAS

These grasslands are flat, open spaces with trees and grass that turn golden during the hot dry season. The wildlife in Kenya's savannas is vanishing due to poaching, human-wildlife conflict, poisoning and legal hunting. You can still see many animals, including: lions, African bush elephants, giraffes, hyenas, African black rhinos, zebras, buffalos, leopards and cheetahs.

FORESTS

There are at least 14 forests found across Kenya. They include montane rainforests, savanna woodlands, dry and coastal forests as well as mangroves. The forests are getting smaller as trees are cut down for farming. They are home to around 778 plant species, as well as a wide range of animals and wildlife, including some of the rarest breeds of butterflies and snakes.

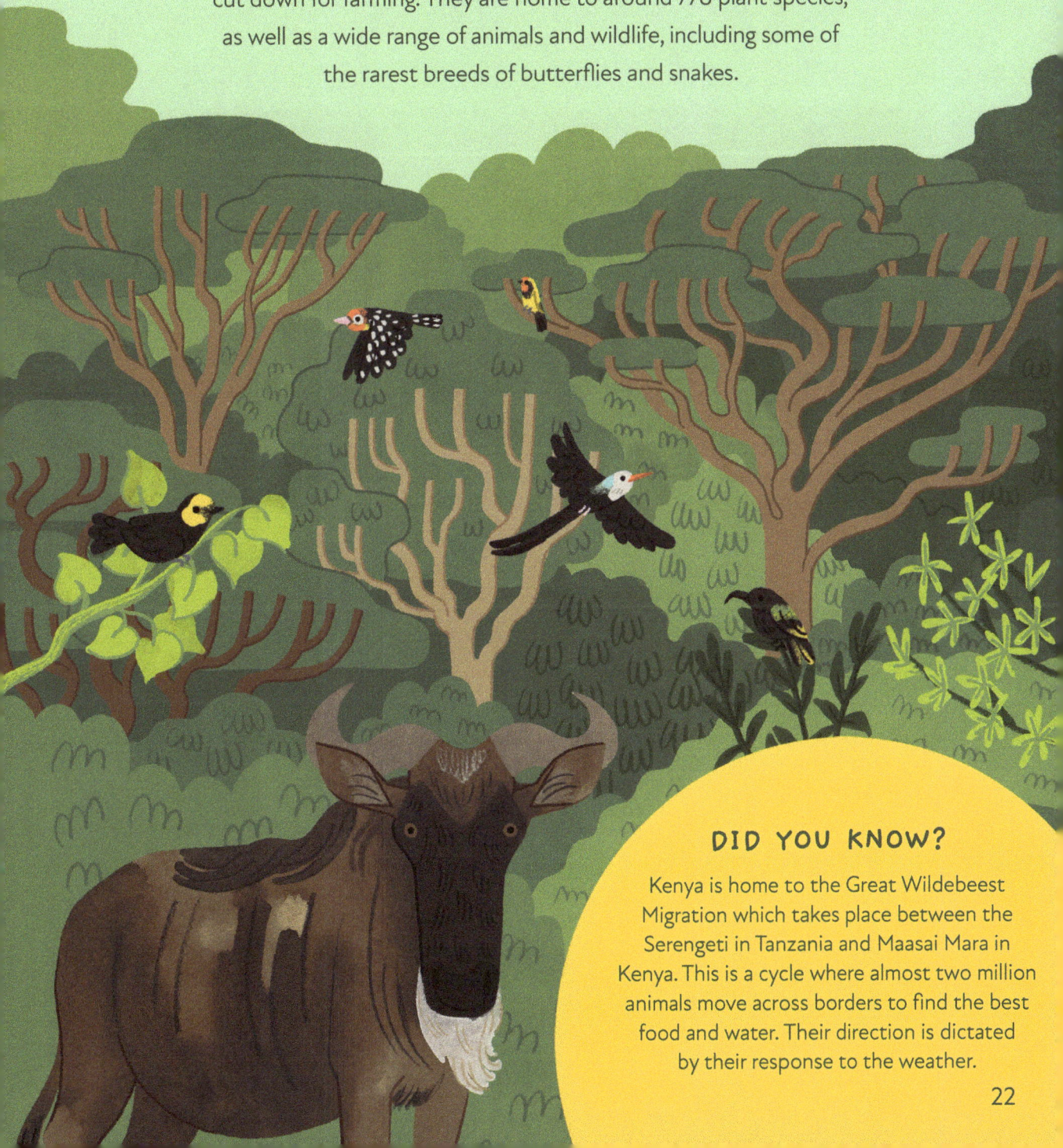

DID YOU KNOW?

Kenya is home to the Great Wildebeest Migration which takes place between the Serengeti in Tanzania and Maasai Mara in Kenya. This is a cycle where almost two million animals move across borders to find the best food and water. Their direction is dictated by their response to the weather.

DESERTS

There are four deserts in Kenya: Chalbi, Kaisut, Mambrui and Nyiri. Kenya's deserts are vast and remote and few people live there. They have rock formations, dunes and harsh winds.

Kaisut Desert

Mambrui Desert

Nyiri Desert

MOORLANDS AND SWAMPS

A moorland is an open habitat, with acid grasslands and swampy landscapes. Yala Swamp, Kenya's largest freshwater wetland, is an important ecosystem. Many different and endangered species live there. It also provides essential resources like water, food and medicine for over 250,000 people.

PLANTS AND TREES

There is a wide variety of trees and plants in Kenya. This includes the umbrella tree, the African cherry and the forest olive, which has a purple-black fruit eaten by birds. Kenya's native trees are very important to the ecosystem.

Trees have a strong cultural significance for communities. Many are seen as sacred and they play a central role in spiritual practices and ceremonies. They inspire storytelling, passing wisdom from one generation to the next, and they are used to produce arts and crafts that showcase Kenya's artistic heritage.

Tree
Mti

FACTS

An African acacia tree can live up to 200 years and can grow to up to 18 m high. There are over 1,300 types of acacia around the world: mostly in Africa and Australia. They are usually found on the savanna flats.

The tree has a substance called "gum arabic" which is used in paints and watercolors, sweets, medicines, printing and dyeing. The wood is also used to make traditional artifacts and carvings.

Their unique umbrella-dome shape allows the trees to capture the most amount of sunlight. It provides shade to wildlife. Acacias protect themselves with their long, sharp thorns, which stop animals from eating their leaves.

THE NAIROBI ORCHID

The orchidaceae is the national flower of Kenya, also known as the "Nairobi Orchid," or the "Nairobi Spider Orchid." It can be found more commonly in the central and western parts of the country and it symbolizes the importance of preserving the country's floral treasures. It is known for its striking appearance, with bright pinkish-purple flowers that resemble spiders.

ANIMALS
Wanyama

Amani and I really enjoy it when Babu and Bibi tell us stories about the different animals in Kenya. They tell us about Kenya's "Ugly five" – marabou stork, hyena, warthog, white-backed vulture and wildebeest – as well as some of the most dangerous animals in Kenya, like the black-backed jackal, and the Nile crocodile.

One day I want to ride an ostrich at the Maasai Ostrich Farm. Ostriches can run up to 60 mph, making it the fastest two-legged creature on earth!

HERE ARE SOME OF THE MANY OTHER ANIMALS YOU MAY FIND IN KENYA – SEE IF YOU CAN SPOT THEM:

Warthog, Little Bee Eater, Hyena, Marabou Stork, Wildebeest, Superb Starling, Common Baboon, Banded Mongoose, Cheetah, Black-Backed Jackal, East African Oryx, White-Backed Vulture, Colobus Monkeys, Waterbuck, Topi, Dik Dik, Reticulated Giraffe, Bushbuck, Lion, Gazelle, Somali Ostrich...

If you are lucky you will spot a Galagos (Bush Baby)!

Babu likes to gather the families in the apartment block some evenings for the elders to tell us all stories. A lot of them are about the people of Kenya, their traditions and beliefs. Mwangi, Zuri and I are inspired to visit some historical landmarks to see some of these things for ourselves. The places we hope to visit one day are:

LAMU OLD TOWN Q

Lamu Old Town is the oldest, best preserved Swahili settlement in East Africa. The city is characterized by narrow streets and magnificent buildings built with coral stone and mangrove timber. The curved doors are beautifully carved. It is the result of a unique fusion of styles.

GEDI RUINS Q

The Gedi ruins are an abandoned city, hidden deep in the tropical forests of Kenya, spread across approximately 45 acres. They are thought to have been built over 800 years ago. Once a 13th-century trading hub, the ruins are now one of the country's great mysteries. No one knows for sure why the town was abandoned.

LEGEND HAS IT...

...that the ruins come alive at night.

CRYING STONE IN KAKAMEGA

The crying stone is a 7 ft-tall structure: one rock sat on top of another, which looks like a head resting on shoulders. A streak of water trickles downwards, making it look like it's crying.

NAIROBI

Nairobi is the biggest city in Kenya, home to over 5.5 million people. A lot of people know it as the "Green City in the Sun." Bibi tells us that the name comes from the Maasai phrase "enkare nyrobi," which means "place of cool waters."

We have only been to Nairobi once. It was so exciting to see the towering skyscrapers and listen to the sound of city-life. Baba says that a lot of people in Kenya want to live in Nairobi because there are lots of business opportunities.

Some great places to see in Nairobi are:

NAIROBI NATIONAL PARK Q

There are over 500 bird species and animals, including buffalo, leopards and wildebeest, as well as over 50 black rhinos, which is the world's largest group of black rhinos. There is also a rescue center in the park which looks after animals that are injured in the wild, and there is an orphanage. It's mainly for young elephants who have lost their families.

MAASAI MARKETS

There are many people who travel to Nairobi just to visit a Maasai market. It is a great place to find souvenirs to take home. You will find anything from pots and pans to handmade artwork, wood carvings, jewelry, shoes and clothes. Bibi loves to haggle at the market, and it was fun to watch her!

RAILWAY MUSEUM

The Railway Museum is right next to the railway station. It was so exciting to see the old locomotive trains that used to run. We enjoyed watching the trains come in and out of the station.

DID YOU KNOW?

Nairobi is the only city in the world that has a national park, which means the park has a backdrop of city skyscrapers and planes coming into land. It is a special place.

LET'S GO TO SCHOOL

Mama and Baba insist we go to school, although we do not have to. We are lucky that elementary school is free. Mwangi, Zuri and I are in second grade and Amani will join first grade next year. We don't start school until we are seven. All of our lessons are taught in English. Not all of my friends at home come with us to school every day.

Our school doesn't have many classrooms, but there is a big field where we run around and play sports. There are not many books in our classroom, but our teachers are creative and sometimes we use bottles, beads and balls to help us with our learning. It makes lessons fun!

SCHOOL
Shule

We walk to and from school together; it takes us almost an hour.
I often run home so I get home quicker to help with chores.

Our cousin, Nduta, is 14 and her school in Nairobi is quite different
to ours as it is much bigger with more classrooms. Her lessons are also
taught in English, but she is learning how to speak in Arabic. Mjomba and
Shangazi are proud of Nduta and they are hoping she will go to university.

Teacher
Mwalimu

Lesson
Somo

Homework
Kazi ya nyumbani

Student
Mwanafunzi

36

WE HAVE THE MOST FUN IN OUR...

MUSIC LESSONS

We play these instruments:

OUD
Udi

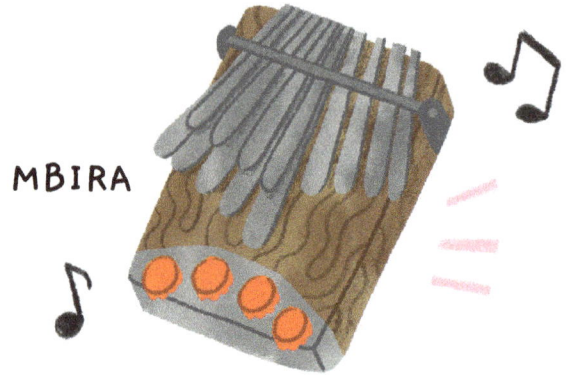

MBIRA

GUITAR
Gitaa

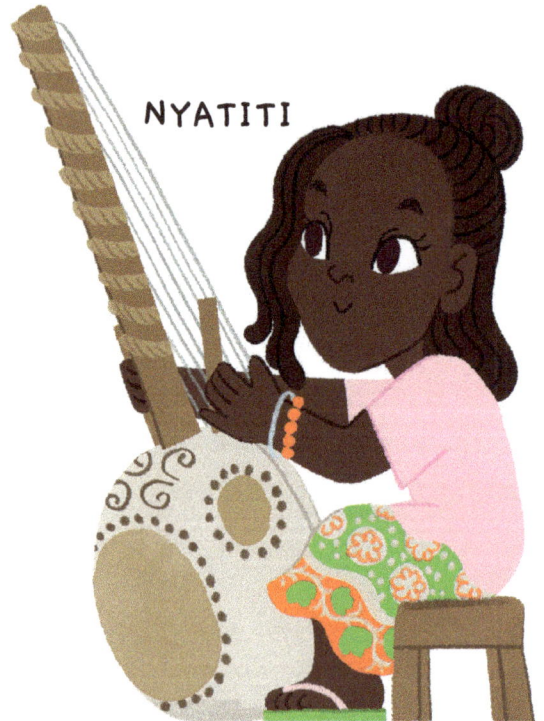

NYATITI

The Kayamba and the Isukuti drum
are also very popular instruments.

PE LESSONS

At school, we play lots of different sports, like soccer and cricket. Soccer is the most popular sport in Kenya, but rugby is also becoming more and more popular.

DID YOU KNOW?

Kenya is home to some of the world's best long-distance runners.

LET'S PLAY

At break time, we like to play soccer and race each other to see who is the fastest. If we are not playing sports, we are playing one of our favorite games, kora.

There must be at least three players. We make a hole in the ground and fill it with 20-30 stones. The first person takes one stone and throws it in the air. Then they try to collect as many stones from the center as they can before the stone falls. If the stone falls to the ground, it is the next player's turn. If they catch the stone, they take another turn and continue to take as many stones from the center as possible. Once all of the stones have gone, the player with the highest number wins. Zuri is competitive and she likes to win every time we play.

Play
Kucheza

LET'S LEARN

NUMBERS
Nambari

Do you know any numbers in Swahili?

We can help you learn to count to ten.

1 MOJA

2 MBILI

3 TATU

4 NNE

Learn
Jifunze

5 TANO

6 SITA

7 SABA

8 NANE

9 TISA

10 KUMI

THE ALPHABET
Herufi

Learning the alphabet is also fun.

How many letters can you say?

A A

B BE

C CHE

D DE

E E

F EF

G GE

H HE

I I

J JE

K KA

L LE
M EM
N EN
O O
P PE
R RE
S SE
T TE
U U
V VE
W WE
Y YE
Z ZE

LET'S SAY

Here are some of our everyday words and phrases.
Why not try and say them?

HOW ARE YOU?

Habari yako?

HOW OLD ARE YOU?

Una umri gani?

MY NAME IS...

Jina langu ni...

I AM ... YEARS OLD

Nina umri wa miaka ...

GOOD MORNING
Habari za Asubuhi

GOOD AFTERNOON
Habari za Mchana

GOOD NIGHT
Usiku Mwema

I LOVE YOU
Nakupenda

THANK YOU
Asante

PLEASE
Tafadhali

LET'S EAT
FOOD & DRINK

KAMAU

I like to have mandazi, which is like a doughnut, and milky tea for breakfast. My favorite dinner is nyama, which is BBQ meat (chicken, goat or beef). I love to eat it with kachumbari. It's a dish of fresh tomato, green chilli and onion salad with herbs and spices, which Mama makes for us when she wants to cook up a feast.

MWANGI

For my breakfast I like to eat mahamri (another type of doughnut) with mbaazi. That's pigeon peas cooked in coconut milk. My favorite dinner is tilapia fry – fried fish.

AMANI

For breakfast I have either uji – a delicious porridge with lemon juice or sweet bananas. For dinner, my favorite is karanga. It's a stew made with beef and potatoes. Bibi loves to make this for us, and sometimes she uses shrimp or chicken.

Our favorite food to eat at school is githeri with avocado.

There are so many delicious snacks that we all love:

Mahindi Choma is roasted corn rubbed with lemon, salt and pepper.

Mutura, a sausage made of goat or cow meat.

Ugali fries, ugali is maize made into dough with water.

Vibibi means "little ladies." They are small, fluffy pancakes made with rice flour and coconut milk.

Mabuyu are the seeds of the baobab fruit coated in a mix of sugar and syrup.

Mango, watermelon, banana, custard apples, jackfruit and orange are all popular fruits.

Falooda is the best milkshake; it is sweet and perfect for a hot day.

Supu is a bone broth which Mama says is good for our health.

Yummy   Eat
Kitamu   Kula

PUBLIC HOLIDAYS

We celebrate lots of public holidays in Kenya. Baba says that we have these days to honor important moments and people in history. We have:

Eid al-Fitr–an Islamic celebration which marks the end of the Muslim month of fasting during Ramadan.

1st May–Labour Day–a day dedicated to recognize the efforts and hard work of Kenya's workers.

1st June–Madaraka Day–this marks the anniversary of Kenyan independence

20th October–Mashujaa Day–is a day to remember Kenya's national heroes.

August–Maralal Camel Derby–aimed at showcasing Samburu's unique history and cultural, ethnic and religious diversity.

November–Mombasa Carnival–the city of Mombasa celebrates Kenyan culture with a carnival.

12th December–Jamhuri Day–Jamhuri means 'republic' in Swahili. The day is set aside to celebrate Kenya becoming independent and establishing a republic in 1964.

We also celebrate birthdays, Easter, Christmas Day, Boxing Day and New Year's Day.

LET'S CELEBRATE

There are many cultural celebrations, including: Rusinga Cultural Festival, Lamu Cultural Festival, Maulidi Cultural Festival and Lake Turkana Cultural Festival. These celebrations display Kenya's heritage, music, dance, food and art.

We LOVE to celebrate! Bibi tells us that festivals and celebrations are a way to keep traditions alive. The whole community will eat, drink, sing and dance together.

CHRISTMAS

Christmas is a lot of fun. We dress the house with balloons, leaves, flowers, ribbons and handmade paper decorations. Our celebrations start on Christmas Eve when we go to church before midnight. We sing carols in English and Swahili. Our favorite is "Christmas naKimangu" (Christmas Mystery). There is also preaching, poetry and dancing, as well as a nativity play.

Once we leave church, we go home and exchange gifts before we go to sleep. Every year, Amani, Cora and I are given a new outfit from Mama and Baba. Sometimes, we go to church again in the morning and when we get home the family prepare the Christmas feast of nyama choma. After church, we visit our friends in the area, and then we continue our celebrations at home, with music, more dancing and more food.

Merry Christmas
Heri ya Krismasi

Happy New Year
Heri ya mwaka mpya

WEDDINGS

Engagements and weddings are big events for the whole community as marriage is seen as a rite of passage to full adulthood. It is tradition for the man, along with his father and uncles, to visit the bride's parents to state his interest in the bride and negotiate a bride price. A bride price is where the groom gives money or livestock to the bride's family before he is given their daughter's hand in marriage.

We go to the fundi (tailor) to get our outfit ready for the celebration. The couple will wear matching colorful clothes. The bride and the groom will typically dress in accordance with tribal traditions. The reception is always a wonderful celebration.

In Kenya some men marry more than one woman.

Happy Birthday
Heri ya siku ya kuzaliwa

Celebrate
Kusherehekea

Party
Karamu

DID YOU KNOW?

Kenyans love tea! You have not been properly welcomed in a Kenyan household if no one has offered you a cup of chai.

KENYA'S TRIBES

There are 42 official tribes in Kenya, with several sub-tribes. Each tribe has their own dialect, rituals, cultural and religious practices, music and dances, food and artistic flair that defines who they are.

Even though the Kikuyu tribe is Kenya's largest, the Maasai tribe is an iconic symbol of Kenyan culture. The Maasai tribe measure their wealth by their cattle and children.

LET'S LISTEN TO A STORY

We are proud of our culture and traditions; they are an important part of our heritage. The elders regularly gather all the children to tell us stories, sharing lessons about life and teaching us about our history. When Zuri's grandma tells us stories, she makes us all laugh until our stomachs hurt.

The "Elephant and Hare" is our favorite. This is a story where the powerful elephant and the cunning hare meet in the forest.

The hare, who is much smaller, challenges the elephant to a race to see who can run the fastest. The confident elephant agrees.

However, knowing he can't outrun the elephant, the hare suggests a race downhill. As they race, the hare tricks the elephant into falling downhill and he crosses the finish line first. The moral of the story is that intelligence can overcome any obstacle. It teaches the importance of not just relying on strength.

Kenyans celebrate important life moments and cultural and religious traditions with joy, camaraderie and a sense of community spirit. Celebrations often vary depending on the ethnic or tribal identity of the communities involved.

GIVING GIFTS

It is common for people to give small gifts such as coffee, sugar, flour or corn when invited to someone's home.

DRESSING UP

Most of the time we wear the same kind of clothes that children wear in the UK. On special occasions, the whole family wears traditional clothes. Each tribe can be recognized by a different fabric and design. Kenyan art is visible in jewelry, clothes and tribal masks. Both men and women tend to wear Sahara boots or sandals.

ENTERTAINMENT

Common forms of local entertainment include traditional dancing, storytelling, bullfighting and stick fighting.

PLAYING MUSIC

We love music and there is always some playing. Our favorite types of music are Kenyan Afropop and reggae. Other popular genres are: benga, ohangla, genge, taarab, kapuka and gospel.

DANCING

We love to have a good time and that usually means there is no music without dancing. Some Kenyan communities perform their traditional dances on special occasions. On a Friday night, most people will be found dancing all night to mugiithi or rhumba. Dances like adumu, mwomboko, isikuti, chakacha and kilumi are the most popular traditional dances; some are performed with the drum and vocals and some do not involve any instruments.

EATING

We eat ugali and nyama choma on special occasions but there is always lots of food to choose from. The bigger the occasion, the bigger the dinner. Mama tells us that the sharing of food is a celebration of culture and connection.

LET'S GET LUCKY

What do you do to cure hiccups? What are the things that bring good luck? Every tribe in Kenya has its own superstitions and traditions. Here are some of them...

HICCUPS

To get rid of hiccups, you should stick your fingers in your ears for 20-30 seconds.

SNEEZING

If someone sneezes, we say "kua" (grow), or "kukuajuu, chinikuna moto" (grow upwards, it is hot below).

BEES CIRCLING

Bees circling the head means news, good or bad, will arrive within two days.

FIREFLIES

If fireflies enter your house at night, you will soon have visitors (Kipsigis superstition).

TWITCHING EYE

When your right eye twitches it means you will see someone that you haven't seen in a long time (Somali superstition).

BAD LUCK

If you come across a cat whilst walking you must turn back and go back home, otherwise it is considered bad luck (Kikuyu superstition).

In almost all Kenyan tribes, seeing an owl is a sign of bad luck.

When your right palm itches, it means you will give out money (Somali superstition).

GOOD LUCK

If you sweep your house in the night, you will chase away your blessings (Luhya superstition).

Wearing a hirizi (a pendant) is believed to bring protection and good fortune.

When your left palm itches it means money will come in.

Luck
Bahati

LET'S DREAM

Sometimes we close our eyes and dream about what we would like to be when we grow up.

Do you know what you would like to be?

Dream
Ndoto

I love to run, and I want to be an athlete. My favorite runner is...

ELIUD KIPCHOGE

Kipchoge is a long-distance runner who is one of the world's greatest marathon runners. He grew up on a farm, and began running long distances as a child when he would jog to and from school. Kipchoge has won two Olympic gold medals and more than ten marathons. He holds the record for running the fastest marathon.

I am at the top of my class in English and I like writing. Baba tells me that he would love to see me become the president one day, like Barack Obama, because he is a good example of how anyone can achieve big dreams through hard work and determination...

BARACK OBAMA

Obama is of Kenyan heritage, born in Hawaii. He was the first black person ever to become the president of the United States, which is a big country far away from here. When he was president, he helped make important decisions for the country, about things like schools, hospitals and how to keep people safe. Before he became president, he was a teacher and a lawyer. Obama is very popular across the world because he always liked to put a smile on people's faces, making sure they felt happy and included.

Amani loves to watch films. She wants to be an actress like...

LUPITA NYONG'O

Lupita is a Kenyan actress who was born in Mexico City and raised in Kenya from the age of three. She is a renowned actress and filmmaker and the first Kenyan and Mexican actress to win an Oscar. She uses her fame for good causes; she has campaigned to protect elephants, for women's health and rights, and to reduce hunger.

Mwangi and Zuri love soccer, their favorite player is...

MICHAEL OLUNGA

Olunga is a well-known soccer player, who was born and raised in Kenya. He started playing soccer as a young boy, but he initially dreamed of being a pilot or an aeronautical engineer. He signed to Tusker soccer club at 19 years old. Olunga is the captain of the Kenya national team. Mwangi wants to be a striker someday, just like him.

Zuri wants to be a businesswoman and admires Vanessa Kingori....

VANESSA KINGORI

Vanessa was born in Kenya and spent time in Saint Kitts in the Caribbean, before moving to London to finish her studies. She is known for her significant contributions to the fashion and media industries. She was the first female publisher of British Vogue magazine and made history by becoming the first black publisher in British Vogue's over-100-year existence. Vanessa is known for amplifying black women's stories and championing inclusivity and diversity.

WE HOPE THAT YOU HAD FUN EXPLORING KENYA WITH US. MWANGI, ZURI, AMANI AND I REALLY ENJOYED SHOWING YOU AROUND. WE HOPE TO SEE YOU BACK SOON!

GOODBYE

KHUSWALA
(LUHYA)

NIINAI
(KIKUYU)

KWAHERI
(SWAHILI)

National anthem

O God of All Creation

Wimbo wa Taifa

MEANING OF THE FLAG

Black   Represents the people of the Republic of Kenya

Red   For the bloodshed during the fight for independence

Green   For the country's landscape and natural wealth

White   Symbolizes peace, honesty, purity and innocence

The black, red and white traditional Maasai shield

The two spears symbolize the defence of these important aspects of Kenyan history and heritage. It also reflects the traditional ways of life in Kenya.

DID YOU KNOW?

Many of the colors and symbolic values are shared with the flag of South Sudan.

HISTORY
Historia

600	Arabs settle in coastal areas
700-1500	Rise of indigenous civilizations
1889	Nairobi railway depot established
1895	British rule of Kenya begins
1944	Kenya African Union formed
1963	Kenya's Independence Day
1964	Republic of Kenya formed with Jomo Kenyatta elected as first president
2004	Wangari Maathai – first African woman to win Nobel Peace Prize
2007	Unrest in the country due to disputed presidential elections
2012	Kenya wildfires
2017	Drought declared a national disaster
2017	New railway line from Mombasa to Nairobi opened
2018	World's last male northern white rhino dies in Kenya
2022	President William Ruto wins election

THE AUTHORS

ANNA MAKANDA

Anna was born in Gweru, Zimbabwe, and raised in London, along with her older sister. Her father is Zimbabwean and her mother, Scottish. Growing up, Anna always dreamed of owning her own business. She started her career as an accountant but soon realized it was time to pursue her dreams. Anna now has her own fitness business. In her spare time, you will find her working on one of her endless ideas or spending time with her family.

SHARMANE BARRETT

Sharmane was born and raised in London, along with her five sisters. Her father is Jamaican and her mother, Trinidadian-English. Growing up, Sharmane was encouraged to pursue a career as a lawyer but after completing her legal studies, she soon realized that law was not for her. She began working in legal recruitment, which gave her an opportunity to live in Singapore for almost four years. Sharmane's passions are travelling and boxing; although these days there is a lot less travelling to exotic destinations, and a lot more time in the gym.

THE ILLUSTRATOR

NATÀLIA JUAN ABELLÓ

Natàlia was born in Barcelona, where she grew up with her older brother, father, and mother. She has loved drawing since she was little and was often found creating and daydreaming as a young girl. Pursuing her dream of working in a creative job, she studied to become a fashion designer but very quickly realized her real passion was to illustrate, especially children's books. She moved to the UK many years ago and she is now happily living in Liverpool. She loves nature, and she's happiest when taking long hikes with her partner and little doggy.

OUR GRATITUDE

We would like to say thank you and extend our gratitude to:

Everyone who helped us with the research: Diana Mwais,
Martin Mwamoni, Doreen Murugi and Elly Omondi for your advice,
opinions and, most importantly, time. Thank you.

Our editor, Amber, our proof-reader, Adam, and Martyn, our wonderful
designer, who not only made our books look as beautiful as they do
but also helped us articulate our vision so perfectly. To our illustrator,
Natàlia, for bringing Kamau, Amani, Mwangi and Zuri to life, and for
showcasing the magic of Kenya.

And not forgetting all our little people for helping us pick the designs
and road-testing the content.

Each other. This is a passion project for us both and to be able to share
this journey with a best friend is the dream.

Anna and Sharmane

LET'S EXPLORE MORE

WWW.OURWORLDMYROOTS.COM

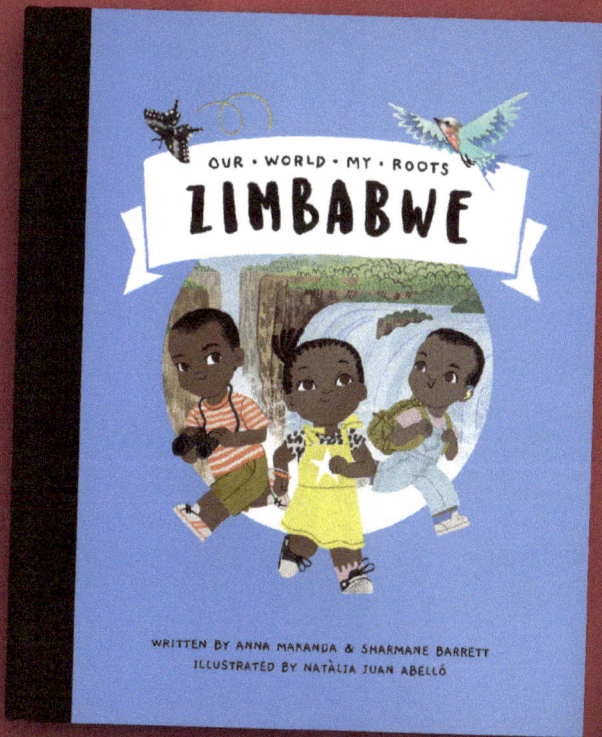

OUR • WORLD • MY • ROOTS
ZIMBABWE

WRITTEN BY ANNA MAKANDA & SHARMANE BARRETT
ILLUSTRATED BY NATÀLIA JUAN ABELLÓ

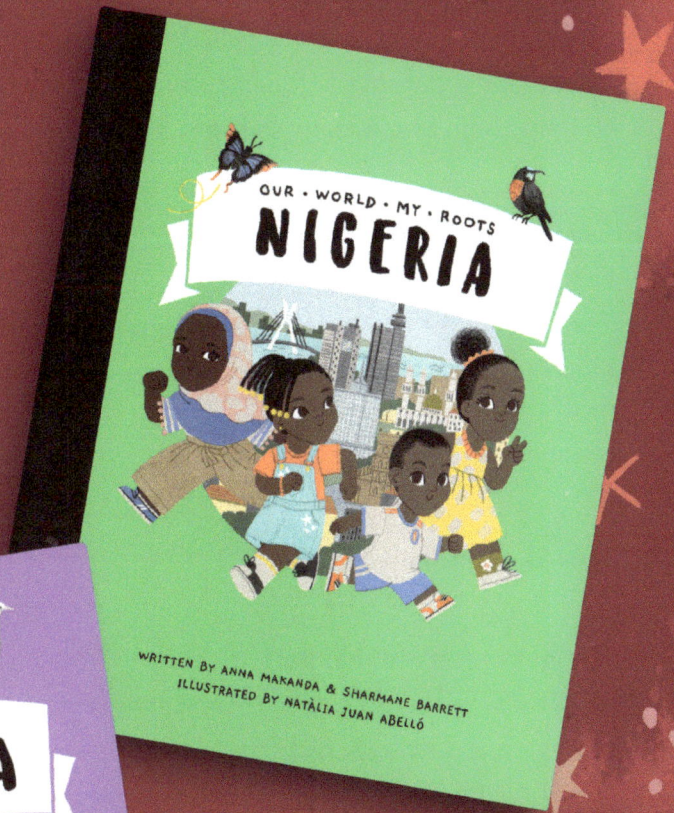

OUR • WORLD • MY • ROOTS
NIGERIA

WRITTEN BY ANNA MAKANDA & SHARMANE BARRETT
ILLUSTRATED BY NATÀLIA JUAN ABELLÓ

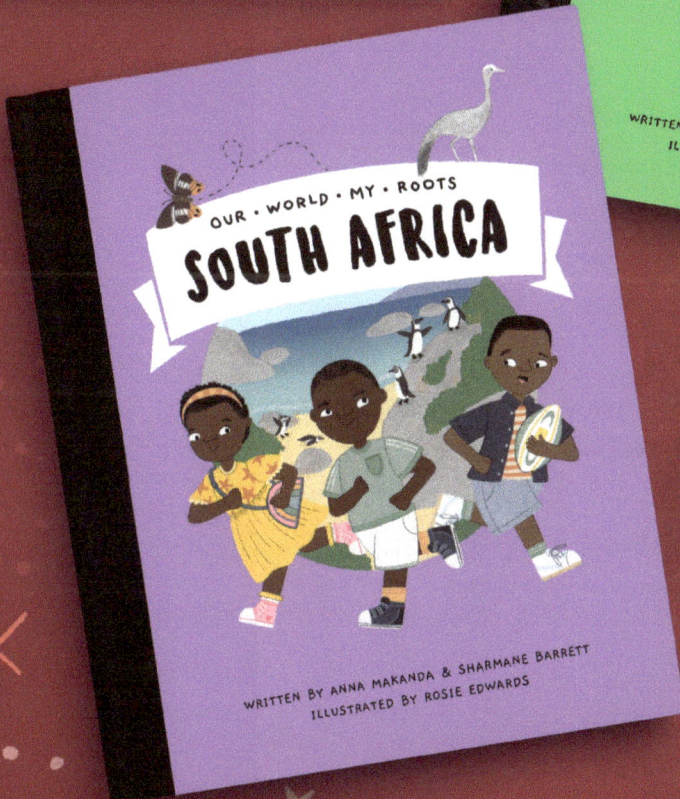

OUR • WORLD • MY • ROOTS
SOUTH AFRICA

WRITTEN BY ANNA MAKANDA & SHARMANE BARRETT
ILLUSTRATED BY ROSIE EDWARDS

OUR MISSION

Our mission is to help ignite a child's interest in their roots and empower them to become culturally confident. We aim to do this by providing parents and caregivers factual yet engaging resources to help them teach their children about their culture and heritage.

COPYRIGHT

A SPECIAL THANKS TO
FLEUR-CLARISSE ATTIVOR,
AGED 10, FOR DRAWING THIS
KENYAN-INSPIRED PATTERN
(WITH THE HELP OF MOMMY).

www.ingramcontent.com/pod-product-compliance
Lightning Source LLC
Chambersburg PA
CBHW060945100426
42813CB00016B/2865